The Super-Duper Seed Surprise

By Nancy I. Sanders
and Susan Titus Osborn

Illustrated by Ronda Krum

With love for my granddaughter Taylor.
May you learn more about Jesus
through reading this book. — S.T.O.

With love for Janice and Bob Shaner.
Thanks for your example of living
and knowing Jesus. — N.I.S.

Parables in Action Series

Lost and Found
Hidden Treasure
Comet Campout
Moon Rocks and Dinosaur Bones
Cooks, Cakes, and Chocolate Shakes
The Super-Duper Seed Surprise

Text copyright © 2000 Nancy I. Sanders and Susan Titus Osborn
Illustrations copyright © 2000 Concordia Publishing House
3558 S. Jefferson Avenue, St. Louis, MO 63118-3968
Manufactured in the United States of America

Library of Congress Catalog-in-Publication Data
Sanders, Nancy I.
    The super-duper seed surprise / Nancy I. Sanders and Susan Titus
Osborn.
        p. cm. — (Parables in action)
Summary: Suzie and her friends plant seeds in their garden and are sur-
prised when the smallest seed produces the biggest, most beautiful tree.
Includes a retelling of Jesus' parable of the mustard seed.
    ISBN 0-570-07113-5
    [1. Seeds—Fiction. 2. Gardens—Fiction. 3. Christian life—Fiction.
    4. Parables.] I. Osborn, Susan Titus, 1944- II. Title.
    PZ7+
    [Fic]—dc21   00-008235

1 2 3 4 5 6 7 8 9 10   09 08 07 06 05 04 03 02 01 00

Hi! My name is Suzie. My friends and I are planting a garden. We've got lots of seeds! Big seeds. Little seeds. Black seeds. Yellow seeds. We'll plant all the seeds in our garden. The seeds will grow into vegetables. We'll give the vegetables to people in a homeless shelter. Our church gives the shelter food.

"Hey, everyone!" Mario shouted. "Come get your seeds." Mario held up three bags of seeds. "Come on, everyone. I have the seeds."

Mario's dog, Woof, wagged his tail and barked. "WOOF!"

Bubbles and I ran toward Mario. "Thanks for the seeds," I said.

"No problem," said Mario. "I sold some dinosaur bones. I used the money to buy seeds. Now we can plant them here in the empty lot."

Mario owns the empty lot. He bought the lot with his own money. He finds dinosaur bones buried in the ground. He sells the bones to the museum. He uses the money for important things. Planting vegetables for the homeless is important.

Mario gave me a bag of green bean seeds to plant. He gave a bag of tomato seeds to Bubbles.

"Thanks!" Bubbles said. She took the seeds. She was dressed like a train engineer. Bubbles does ads on TV. She always practices for them.

"What are you practicing for today?" I asked.

"For a Trent the Train Engine ad," she said. "It's a new toy train that kids can buy."

The Spy finished writing his
spy notes. He closed his spy
book. SLAM. He walked toward
Mario. He held out his hand.
Mario gave him a bag of corn
seeds.

"What seeds are you going to
plant?" I asked Mario.

Mario held up a teeny, tiny
seed.

I looked at it. Bubbles
looked too. So did The Spy.

"Ark, ark! Bam, bam!" said
The Spy. He wrote more notes
in his spy book.

9

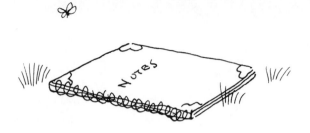

I knew what he said. I'd been around The Spy a long time. "Ark, ark! Bam, bam!" was his secret code for "Wow!" The Spy liked to talk in secret code.

"Wow!" said Bubbles.

"What kind of seed is that?" I asked Mario. "That's the smallest seed I've ever seen."

"I don't know," Mario said. "I found it on the floor at the seed store. The lady said I could keep it. She didn't know what it was either."

"Let's plant it and find out," I said.

Bubbles blew a loud blast on her train whistle. "All aboard!" she shouted. "It's time to start. Let's plant our seeds."

For the rest of the day, we worked hard. We dug deep holes in the dirt. We planted the seeds. We covered them with dirt.

Mario planted his teeny, tiny seed in the middle of the garden. He helped us plant our seeds. Soon we were done. The Spy sat down and wrote spy notes.

Bubbles blew on her train whistle. "Choo! Choo! Next stop is my house!" she shouted. "All aboard for snacks!"

"Let's have chocolate shakes," I said. One time we made chocolate shakes. We also cooked a birthday cake. It was

for our teacher, Mr. Zinger.

"Shakes! Sounds yummy,"
Bubbles said. "We'll use The
Spy's recipe. It's the best!"

The Spy held up his spy book.
The recipe for chocolate shakes
was there.

We got in line behind Bubbles.
She handed each of us a ticket.
"All aboard!" she shouted.

"Chugga, chugga! Choo, choo!"
we said together.

Off we went to Bubbles' house
to make chocolate shakes.

Woof ran ahead of us. He
barked. "WOOF!"

The next day we met at the empty lot after school.

"Where did that tree come from?" Bubbles asked. She pointed to the middle of the garden.

"I don't know," I said. "It wasn't there yesterday."

The Spy opened his spy book. He wrote spy notes.

Mario said, "That's funny. How could a tree grow in one day? In the middle of my empty lot?"

Bubbles pointed to the right.

"I planted tomatoes over there," she said.

I pointed to the left.

"I planted green beans over there," I said.

The Spy pointed to another place. He had planted corn there.

"Where did you plant your
seed, Mario?" I asked.

Mario pointed to the middle of
the empty lot. He pointed to the
tree. "I planted my seed in the
middle, right where that tree is."

"Wow!" I said. "Your teeny, tiny
seed grew into a tree."

Woof ran around the garden. He stopped. He looked up at the tree. He barked. "WOOF! WOOF! WOOF!"

"What is it, Woof?" Mario shouted. We all ran toward the tree.

"WOOF! WOOF! WOOF!"

"Hey!" Mario shouted. "The tree is growing bigger!"

"Ark, ark! Bam, bam!" shouted The Spy.

"Wow!" Bubbles and I shouted.

The tree grew bigger and bigger right in front of our eyes. It grew more branches. It grew more leaves. It grew taller and taller.

Soon it was as tall as Mr. Zinger. What a surprise!

It grew even more branches. It grew even more leaves. It grew taller and taller and taller.

Soon it was as tall as a house! What an even bigger surprise!

"Ark, ark! Bam, bam!"
The Spy shouted again. He
wrote lots of spy notes.

Just then Mr. Zinger
walked up. "Hi, Larry. Hi,
Nan," he said. "Hi, Mario
and Susan."

Mr. Zinger is our teacher.
He's the best. He always
calls us by our real names.
The Spy's real name is Larry.
Bubbles' real name is Nan.
My real name is Susan.

"I was walking home
after school," Mr. Zinger said.
"I heard you kids shouting.
I came over to see what was
happening."

Mr. Zinger stood next to the
tree. He looked high up in the
air.

"Where did this tree come
from?" Mr. Zinger asked. "What
kind of tree is it? It's the
biggest tree I've ever seen."

30

We told Mr. Zinger every-
thing. We told him how Mario
planted a teeny, tiny seed. Mr.
Zinger was really surprised!

Mr. Zinger gave a low whistle.
"Wow," he said. "That's quite a
tree!"

Mario jumped up and down. "Look! Look!" He pointed to the tree. "Apples and oranges are growing on the tree! Both at the same time!"

"Ark, ark! Bam, bam!" shouted The Spy. He was excited. He even forgot to write spy notes!

We watched the tree. It grew more red apples and big oranges. Wow!

Just then a noisy flock of birds flew in. "Squawk! Squawk!" they shouted. Tall, blue birds landed on the branches. They started making nests.

"Those are the most beautiful birds I've ever seen!" I said.

"What are they?" Bubbles asked.

"They are peacocks," said Mr. Zinger in surprise.

Other kinds of birds flew in.
They landed on the branches.
They made nests too.

"Squawk! Squawk! Squawk!"

"Tweet, tweet, tweet!"

"Chirp, chirp, chirp."

A lady from the museum came by. "I heard a flock of peacocks. They flew over the museum." She pointed to the big tree. "How did that tree get here?"

We told her about Mario's teeny, tiny seed. We told her how it grew into the biggest tree in the world.

Crowds of people came. They all wanted to see the huge tree and the beautiful birds. Bubbles lined them up. She gave them tickets to take turns. We told everyone what happened. The Spy took lots of spy notes.

40

It started to get dark.
It was time to go home.

"Thanks for coming," I
said. "Thanks for sharing our
super-duper seed surprise!"

Bubbles blew a loud blast
on her train whistle. "All
aboard!" she shouted.

Everyone cheered. "Good-
bye!"

43

The Parable of the Mustard Seed

Based on Matthew 13:31–32

One day, Jesus told a parable:

God's kingdom is like a mustard seed. The mustard seed is the smallest seed a farmer plants. But it grows so big that birds come to nest in its branches.

The seed Mario planted was like a mustard seed. Although it was little, it grew into a big, beautiful tree. Birds made their homes in its branches.

Just like the mustard seed, we might feel small. But when we believe in Jesus and are part of God's kingdom, our faith makes us important. God will help us work together with one another and do big things for Him.

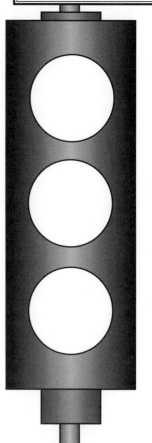

Hi, everyone! God thinks you're very important! Although you may be small, your faith helps you do big things for God. Here's one way you can put Jesus' Parable of the Mustard Seed into ACTION!

Parables In Action

Get Ready. Find a branch without leaves that has many smaller branches extending from it. Gather an empty flowerpot, plastic wrap, plaster of paris, a plastic spoon, a large paper cup, construction paper, markers, tape, and wrapped hard candy.

Get Set. Line the pot with plastic wrap. Ask an adult to help mix the plaster of paris with water in the cup. Stir until it is thick, then pour it into the flowerpot. Stand the branch in the plaster so it looks like a small tree.

Go! Decorate your tree with paper leaves, pictures of birds, and paper fruit. Tape wrapped hard candies on the branches. When your friends visit, invite them to pick a piece of candy from the tree. Tell them about Jesus and the Parable of the Mustard Seed.